FRESH: REVIVING STALE FAITH
Kerry Shook

Small-Group Experience written by
Jason Jaggard

Fresh: Reviving Stale Faith
Small-Group Study Guide
Published by LifeWay Press®
©2011 Kerry Shook

ISBN 978-1-4158-7211-6
Item 005470700

Dewey Decimal Classification: 248.3
Subject Headings: MEDITATION \ FASTING \ SPIRITUAL LIFE

Unless otherwise noted, all Scripture references are taken from the Holy Bible, New International Version, copyright © 1973, 1978, 1984 by International Bible Society. Used by permission. Scriptures marked NRSV are from the New Revised Standard Version of the Bible, copyright © 1989 by the Division of Christian Education of the National Council of Churches of Christ in the United States of America. Used by permission. All rights reserved. Scriptures marked The Message are from The Message, copyright © 1993, 1994, 1995, 1996, 2001, 2002 by Eugene Peterson. Published by NavPress. Used by permission.

To order additional copies of this resource, order online at *www.lifeway.com;* write LifeWay Small Groups; One LifeWay Plaza; Nashville, TN 37234-0175; fax order to (615) 251-5933; or call toll-free (800) 458-2772.

Printed in the United States of America

Leadership and Adult Publishing
LifeWay Church Resources
One LifeWay Plaza
Nashville, TN 37234-0175

CONTENTS

BEHIND THE CURTAIN

There are times in every Christ-follower's life when our passion for God begins to wane and our faith starts to get stale. This study came out of such an experience in my walk with God. I felt like God was distant, and I was just going through the motions in my spiritual life.

Ironically enough, I found a fresh and renewed relationship with God when I began to lean into ancient, spiritual disciplines. As I began to practice these time-honored biblical disciplines, my relationship with God became more intimate and personal, and His Word became alive!

Contemporary Christianity has all but abandoned the ancient spiritual disciplines of meditation, fasting, and silence. And as a result we've given way to overcrowded schedules and burnout. I pray that this study will help you hit the refresh button on your faith and experience a new and fresh joy in your journey with Jesus.

Blessings,

Kerry

Kerry Shook

ABOUT THIS STUDY

Welcome to *Fresh: Reviving Stale Faith*—a small-group Bible study from the *Platform* series. In this small-group experience, pastor Kerry Shook explores the ancient disciplines of meditation, fasting, and silence and examines how patterns of the past are actually practices that promise to revive a stale faith.

Here are the elements you'll be encountering during this small-group experience:

- **Warm Up** – a time for sharing stories
- **Video Set Up** – establishes context for your small-group time
- **Viewer Guide** – integral points from the video message to enhance discussion
- **Biblical Background** – biblical insight for greater understanding
- **Scripture** – all primary Scriptures are printed in the study guide
- **Small-Group Questions** – application, self-revelation, interpretation, or observation (discovery Bible study method builds community, invites God in, and generates transformational discussion)
- **Journal** – contributes to personal devotional time
- **You're Up** – a challenge for group members to practice what they have learned
- **Leader Notes** - in colored text at the beginning of each section

The Art of Focus

We love things that are fresh. From fresh food at the farmer's market down the street to a fresh idea that makes us think about the world in a new way—fresh gives a sense of life, of enjoyment, of fulfillment. When we get off a plane and take our first breath of fresh air, it just feels good. Our bodies actually long for freshness. Fresh food and fresh air are simply better for us.

In the same way, our souls long for the freshness of life. All of us have experienced a moment or two when life just seemed more full, more rewarding, more ... fresh. The question is, how can the word *fresh* describe our lifestyle rather than just a moment in our lives?

In this session we will be looking at the benefits of practicing the discipline of meditation. Is it possible that in focusing our minds on the right things, our passion for God can be renewed and our faith revived?

WARM UP

Try not to spend too much time here, but let everyone answer the warm-up questions. Getting group members involved early helps create the best small-group environment. If this is the first time the group is meeting, make sure everyone works on learning names.

What's your favorite thing to have fresh? Maybe it's a food. Maybe a drink. Maybe an experience or a place or a relationship.

Think of a time in your life when things felt fresh for you. Tell the group about it.

VIDEO SET UP

The information below sets up the video. It can be read aloud to the group, read by group members ahead of time, or group members can read the information silently while the facilitator sets up the video. As you watch the video, encourage the group to follow Kerry's instruction to underline, circle, or interact with the key words in the passages.

Sometimes the path to something new is paved with ancient stones. Kerry points out in this video session that a great paradox of spirituality is the old creating the new—that the key to living a fresh faith is found in spiritual disciplines that have been around for thousands of years. In order to move forward with our lives perhaps we have to look back, to examine the ancient practices that will lead us into the life with God that we truly long for.

This first session looks at one of those ancient practices: the discipline of meditation. Meditation can feel unproductive. It's hard to justify getting up early or sacrificing time to just contemplate or listen or read an ancient book. As our lives become busier and busier, the idea of meditation can seem less and less practical.

So, is meditation a waste of time? If there are any benefits to meditation, what are they?

Take a moment to read through the Scriptures on page 12 before watching "The Art of Focus" (11:13). Then discuss the two questions designed as follow-up to the video on the Viewer Guide page.

SHOW VIDEO NOW.

VIEWER GUIDE

Included are two questions designed as follow-up to "The Art of Focus." This time is set aside for discussion within the group about what they heard, how it affected them, and possible applications. These questions may be only a beginning. Feel free to begin the conversation by asking what thoughts, insights, or stories had the most impact on group members.

1. At the beginning of his video message, Kerry mentions some misconceptions about meditation. When you think of meditation, what immediately comes to your mind?

2. Kerry mentions three benefits of meditation: a secure mind, a productive life, and a fresh faith. Which of those resonates with you most? Why?

BIBLICAL BACKGROUND

With music there is usually a story behind the song that helps listeners appreciate the heart and soul behind both the music and the lyrics. Scripture is no different. Below you'll find a brief story behind this week's Scripture intended to provide additional understanding and insight.

Psalm 1 is the primary text for this week's conversation on meditation. The Psalms are a collection of songs written by various authors, many by Israel's greatest king, David. The psalms are passionate, emotional, and raw pieces of art that use beautiful and sometimes powerful imagery and poetic language to capture the authentic ups and downs of life and how we interact with it.

The part of the world where these songs were written was dry and hot. The desert of the ancient Middle East made a stark contrast to the image of a blessed man portrayed by the writer of Psalm 1. In the midst of scorching heat and a brutal sun, a blessed man is "like a tree planted by streams of water" (v. 3). Water was a commodity—precious and valuable. It was and is the vital source of life for the Middle East and the rest of the world.

In this way, the psalmist uses this imagery to evoke the emotions of thirst and desperation as well as security, productivity, and strength. It acknowledges the hostile environments we sometimes find ourselves and our faith in and yet reminds us that the Stream of water is always available for us to plant ourselves near, if we are only willing.

SCRIPTURE

¹ Blessed is the man who does not walk in the counsel of the wicked or stand in the way of sinners or sit in the seat of mockers. ² But his delight is in the law of the LORD, and on his law he meditates day and night. ³ He is like a tree planted by streams of water, which yields its fruit in season and whose leaf does not wither. Whatever he does prospers.
– Psalm 1:1-3

⁹ How can a young man keep his way pure? By living according to your word. ¹⁰ I seek you with all my heart; do not let me stray from your commands. ¹¹ I have hidden your word in my heart that I might not sin against you. ¹² Praise be to you, O LORD; teach me your decrees. ¹³ With my lips I recount all the laws that come from your mouth. ¹⁴ I rejoice in following your statutes as one rejoices in great riches. ¹⁵ I meditate on your precepts and consider your ways. ¹⁶ I delight in your decrees; I will not neglect your word.
– Psalm 119:9-16

SMALL-GROUP QUESTIONS

Over the next few pages you'll find discussion questions, material that may be used as additional discussion points, and a journal exercise for group members to complete away from the group.

> **"Biblical meditation is not emptying your mind with meaningless words. Biblical meditation is filling your mind with the meaningful Word of God."**

1. At any given time, we're meditating on something. Our minds constantly hum with the day-to-day needs of our lives. What things (good, bad, both) do we tend to fill our minds with?

2. How do you see these things affecting your life?

A PERSONAL BENT

The Bible has always been a little intimidating to me (Jason). It's a big book. It has weird names and strange places. When I was 10 years old I didn't feel like I understood much of it, yet I was told it was important and was encouraged to read it. If I had a dollar for every time I fell asleep at night praying or reading the Bible as a teenager, I could have paid my way through college.

As I grew older, I discovered that there are many different ways to interact with this sacred text. Some people love reading large portions at a time. Others love to read just one verse. Some people use a plan; other people tend to skip around. Some people love to get deep into the commentaries and theological discussions. Others have friends (just kidding).

I have discovered that, depending on the season of my life and faith, I read the Scriptures differently. Sometimes I just want to swim in the stories and read whole New Testament letters like I would read an e-mail from an old friend. Other times I cling to one verse like a life raft as I go through a difficult time. Sometimes the Scriptures come alive. And sometimes they seem stale.

Sounds like a relationship, right? It is. Interacting with the Scriptures is a cornerstone for us interacting with God. There are a million ways to do it; the only wrong way is to not do it at all.

"The person who meditates on God's Word is planted when everything else around is getting uprooted … [they have] a depth in their soul that won't be affected by the evening news."

3. Kerry notes that one of the benefits to meditating on Scripture is a "secure mind." How might you display an insecure mind from time to time?

4. How do you see meditating on the promises of Scripture connect with having more peace in the day-to-day affairs of living?

"There's a big difference between activity and productivity."

5. Activity comes from doing things that are instantly available. Productivity comes from doing the things that matter. All of us tend to forget what's important from time to time and get consumed by things that don't matter as much. How do you think meditating on the Scriptures helps you focus on what matters versus what's available?

STUFF THAT MAKES YOU SMART

"Feelings follow action" is one of the hardest concepts to grasp in life. We want things to feel good all the time, and when they don't we think either the action is wrong or we're wrong for wanting the action. We struggle to believe that our choices can change the way we feel. Yet a breakthrough area of genetic research shows just how powerful our choices are. *Epigenetics* is the study of how our choices and environment affect our DNA. Contrary to the belief that our DNA is our destiny, it is now being discovered that our choices can actually turn on and off certain parts of our genome and affect not only our own destiny but also shape the destiny of our children and our children's children. [1] Put simply: our choices are more powerful than we ever imagined.

"In the Hebrew, [*prosperity*] literally means the ability to make wise decisions. ... Decisions determine your destiny."

6. Reread Psalm 1:3. Kerry refers to the ability to make wise decisions as "one of the greatest gifts you could ever have." How would you describe the connection between meditating on God's Word and the ability to make wise decisions?

7. What does this ability mean to you and how do you see it affecting all aspects of your life—family, career, friends?

8. Psalms 1:1-3 and 119:9-16 use the word "delight." When we delight in something, our thoughts constantly turn to it, it makes us smile, and it cheers our hearts. How might relating to the Lord and His Word in this way transform your view of meditation and the time you spend with Him and in His Word?

9. Maybe this concept of meditation is new to you. Or maybe you're just looking at it in a different way now. So, how important is a fresh, alive, vibrant faith to you? How will you take responsibility for refreshing your own faith?

JOURNAL

This journaling opportunity is designed for group members to utilize at another time. They may choose to answer the questions in the space provided or they may prefer to use the space and time to take a deep question or concern to God.

What are some of the obstacles that keep you from mediating on the Scriptures more? List your obstacles below and for each one, write a way you can overcome that obstacle in order to practice the art of meditation more in your daily life.

YOU'RE UP

Spiritual practices aren't meant to be simple tasks that we check off of our to-do lists so we can be right with God. Consider the following points as you seek to interact with God in a more intimate and intentional way:

- Meditating with God can help you have a more secure, peaceful mind.

- Meditating with God can help you be more productive.

- Meditating with God can help you begin tapping into a fresh faith.

- The spiritual disciplines won't always be enjoyable, yet we can enjoy the benefits that they offer.

- Let your choices shape your desires, not the other way around.

Spend some time this week reading the Word. Take all pressure off to do it "right." Just open your Bible and see what happens.

In the next session we will continue to look at the first half of Psalm 1 and dive into some practical ways we can pray and meditate on God's Word. To prepare for the lesson, take a few minutes to reread Psalm 1:1-3. Also look at Exodus 16:4-5,19.

1. John Cloud, "Why Your DNA Isn't Your Destiny," *Time* [online] 6 Jan. 2010 [cited 12 Sept. 2011]. Available on the Internet: *www.time.com*.

The Art of Discipline

Have you ever wanted to do something but just didn't know how to do it? Maybe it was learning to play an instrument or learning how to cook. When we were kids we were taught how to do stuff all the time—someone showed us how to tie our shoes and how to make our beds. As we grow older, life becomes more complicated and the things we try to accomplish become more important: how to have great relationships or how to be a responsible employee. We want to do these things well but sometimes we need help. The same is true for our spiritual lives. Many of us want to grow spiritually but we need a few pragmatic tips to point us in the right direction.

This week we're going to look at the strategy for meditation. But don't misunderstand. It *is* a discipline, but it's *not* all about a checklist you complete. It's about a relationship. A living, breathing, dynamic, *fresh* relationship with God and His Word.

WARM UP

Try not to spend too much time here, but let everyone answer the warm-up question. Getting group members involved early helps create the best small-group environment.

Think of a time when someone showed you how to do something. Maybe it was a teacher in school or a mentor or a pastor. Maybe you were learning to play a sport or learning something on the job. What are your most vivid memories of that experience?

VIDEO SET UP

The information below sets up the video. It can be read aloud to the group, read by group members ahead of time, or group members can read the information silently while the facilitator sets up the video. As you watch the video, encourage the group to follow Kerry's instruction to underline, circle, or interact with the key words in the passages.

The first followers of Jesus asked Him to teach them how to pray (Luke 11:1). Jesus followed in a long rabbinical tradition of modeling healthy spirituality and passing it on to His followers. Looking to others who have been following Jesus for longer than us is a great way to continue to grow in our own spiritual development. Sometimes we learn from our parents or pastors or books or people we've never met. These mentors help put flesh and bone to abstract ideas like prayer and meditation. In showing us how they do it, they help us discover how we can do it.

In this week's video session, Kerry opens us up to his own spiritual journey, the wisdom of the Scriptures, and some spiritual forefathers of the faith. Kerry shares practical insights and helpful tips on how he likes to meditate on the Scriptures—what works for him and what has worked for others—in hopes that we can begin to meditate on the Scriptures ourselves on a daily basis.

Take a moment to read through the Scriptures on page 26 before watching "The Art of Discipline" (14:43). Then discuss the two questions designed as follow-up to the video on the Viewer Guide page.

SHOW VIDEO NOW.

VIEWER GUIDE

Included are two questions designed as follow-up to "The Art of Discipline." This time is set aside for discussion within the group about what they heard, how it affected them, and possible applications. These questions may be only a beginning. Feel free to begin the conversation by asking what thoughts, insights, or stories had the most impact on group members.

1. In his video message, Kerry shared his method for meditating on Scripture. What are the 4 Rs?

2. What are some of the tips Kerry gave to help us "squeeze all of the nutrients" out of a passage?

BIBLICAL BACKGROUND

With music there is usually a story behind the song that helps listeners appreciate the heart and soul behind both the music and the lyrics. Scripture is no different. Below you'll find a brief story behind this week's Scripture intended to provide additional understanding and insight.

Kerry identifies two primary passages in his video message this week. First, he revisits Psalm 1:1-3 from last week. This particular Psalm uses what's called a "parallel structure"—essentially saying the same thing multiple times but in different ways. It's an artistic way to create a larger space for readers to reflect on an important idea that they might miss if they were to just see or read the content once and move on. The gist of the passage is to be aware of who is influencing us and to not be influenced by people whose lives don't reflect the values of God.

The second Scripture Kerry identifies is from Exodus 16 and talks about how the people of Israel were able to eat while they were wandering through the desert for 40 years. Kerry elaborates on the idea of manna from heaven. The word *manna* in the Hebrew literally means, "What is it?" or could even be translated as "stuff." It was not an affectionate title.

Manna became a theme throughout the Hebrew and Christian Scriptures as a metaphor for God's provision. A gold jar of manna was kept in the ark of the covenant so the Israelites would remember that it is God who provided for them (Hebrews 9:4). In Revelation 2:17 John writes that those who follow Jesus are given "hidden manna"—unseen nourishment as part of their relationship with God.

SCRIPTURE

¹ Blessed is the man who does not walk in the counsel of the wicked or stand in the way of sinners or sit in the seat of mockers. ² But his delight is in the law of the LORD, and on his law he meditates day and night. ³ He is like a tree planted by streams of water, which yields its fruit in season and whose leaf does not wither. Whatever he does prospers.
– Psalm 1:1-3

⁴ Then the LORD said to Moses, "I will rain down bread from heaven for you. The people are to go out each day and gather enough for that day. In this way I will test them and see whether they will follow my instructions. ⁵ On the sixth day they are to prepare what they bring in, and that is to be twice as much as they gather on the other days." …
¹⁹ Then Moses said to them, "No one is to keep any of it until morning." – Exodus 16:4-5,19

²² Do not merely listen to the word, and so deceive yourselves. Do what it says. ²³ Anyone who listens to the word but does not do what it says is like a man who looks at his face in a mirror ²⁴ and, after looking at himself, goes away and immediately forgets what he looks like.
– James 1:22-24

SMALL-GROUP QUESTIONS

Over the next few pages you'll find discussion questions, material that may be used as additional discussion points, and a journal exercise for group members to complete away from the group.

"You do what's right whether you feel like it or not and the feelings come along because feelings always follow actions."

1. Kerry notes that spiritual disciplines don't always feel good and yet they're still important. What are some other things in life that are important to do whether we feel like doing them or not?

"Christianity is not a set of rules; it's a relationship. ... That's why the strategy is personal."

2. It's easy for things to become legalistic or lifeless. What do you see as the benefits of continuing to push through with spiritual disciplines even when you don't feel like it?

REEL TRUTH

The film *Big Fish* tells the story of a relationship between a larger-than-life dad who is dying and his increasingly cynical son. The dad had been known to tell a few tall tales about his own life—it was often hard to know fact from fiction. All the son wanted was to know the truth about his father's life. He had heard the stories so many times that they had become stale. Toward the end of the film you'll hear this narration from the son: "Have you ever heard a joke so many times that you've forgotten why it's funny? But then you hear it again and suddenly it's new. You remember why you loved it in the first place." (Sony Pictures, 2003)

The same struggle can come for anyone who has been around the story of God for very long. Sometimes we hear the truth so many times that instead of it becoming more powerful in our lives, it becomes more rote or static. We can lose sight of the impact through overexposure, just like a favorite joke or even an old relationship; we have to remember why we loved it in the first place.

"If I enjoy the Lord I'm going to spend time with Him and I'm going to make sure that I cherish that time."

3. Who are the people in your life you most cherish and enjoy spending time with? How do you make your time together intentional and meaningful?

4. In what ways do those relationships parallel the time you spend with the Lord? How do they differ?

5. Consider the concept of creating a sacred place or sacred space for meditating on God's Word. How might creating a time, place, or activity that you regularly share with the Lord refresh your relationship with Him?

"You haven't meditated until you live it out."

6. Reread James 1:22-24. You can memorize Scripture and spend time with God every day, but if your life isn't changing then you aren't maximizing the power and discipline of meditation. What are some practical ways we can make sure we're immersing ourselves in the Scriptures versus simply memorizing the words?

7. What is an example of a time when you truly let God's Word transform your actions? How did it affect your faith?

FAITH IN HISTORY

David Koresh—a cult leader and central figure behind the 76 deaths in the 1993 Waco, Texas tragedy—had large portions of the Bible memorized by the age of 12. Joseph Stalin was a seminary student before becoming a tyrannical and murderous dictator. More than simply knowing the Bible, you have to let it shape you into who God is calling you to be. More inspiring examples are the likes of Martin Luther King, Jr. or Mother Teresa. Ironically, Gandhi is often quoted as saying, "I like your Christ. I do not like your Christians. They are so unlike your Christ."

"Some of you have been depending on manna you got 10 years ago. … Some of you have been depending on manna you got last spring, and your faith now is stale."

8. Look at the Exodus 16 passage again. Daily life is a school of faith for us just as surely as the wilderness was for Israel—a school of faith in which we are invited to learn to trust completely in God. How are you at trusting Jesus as your manna—at meeting your needs?

9. Experiencing God is always only a choice away. Is there a gap in your life between hearing from God and obeying God? How can you begin today to allow the truth of His Word to penetrate the nooks of your life in order for you to live a life of fresh faith?

JOURNAL

This journaling opportunity is designed for group members to utilize at another time. They may choose to answer the question in the space provided or they may prefer to use the space and time to take a deep question or concern to God.

How do you feel about the benefits of reinvesting time into studying and applying the Scriptures to your life? Maybe you're not sure how to fit it into your schedule. Maybe the concept challenges your faith. Maybe you know God is calling you to some new act but you're afraid of what might happen. Take a few moments to journal about those feelings. Be honest with yourself and with God. Ask Him to help you work past your doubts and fears so that you can fully experience the fresh faith that comes through meditating on His Word.

YOU'RE UP

To discover the Scriptures in a fresh way, remember the following:

- The strategy for Scripture meditation is personal. You have to find a way that works for you.

- The secret to meditating on God's Word is daily interaction.

- You haven't truly meditated until you've sincerely applied it.

Use this next week to begin working on how you want to interact with the Scriptures on a daily basis. Set up a sacred place. Commit to the practice daily—whether you feel like it or not. Ask God to help you apply what He's showing you. And most of all, enjoy the experience.

In the next session we will talk about the ancient art of fasting as a means for keeping our faith fresh. To prepare for the lesson, take a few minutes to read Matthew 6:16-18; Luke 9:23; Matthew 4:4; and 1 Samuel 7:6.

The Art of Restraint

Most of us love to eat. Fine dining or fast food. Four-star restaurants or ordering by number. Steak or hamburgers. Enchiladas or pizza. Sushi or egg rolls. And of course, dessert! Eating is one of the most universal pleasures shared by humanity. So why in the world would anyone intentionally fast not eat? Why deny ourselves the pleasure? Why deny our bodies the nourishment? In a culture where the word *denial* isn't necessarily seen as a virtue, how could something positive come from it?

This week we're going to begin a discussion about the purpose and power of fasting—how going without food can actually feed our souls, fill our spirits, and keep our faith fresh and vibrant.

WARM UP

Try not to spend too much time here, but let everyone answer the warm-up question. Getting group members involved early helps create the best small-group environment.

What's your very favorite thing to eat? Try and describe it to the group in the most tantalizing terms and tones, like a commercial selling chocolate to women.

VIDEO SET UP

Restraint and self-denial are perhaps two of the best-kept secrets of an extraordinary life, yet we all have to deny ourselves certain things. To work at one location is to *not* work somewhere else. To marry one person is to *not* marry someone else. To choose is to limit. To accept one thing is to deny other things.

Some people have learned to leverage self-denial to aid them in their goals. From athletes to monks, people who are successful know that they have to deny short-term pleasure for long-term gain. Yet the simple spiritual discipline of fasting—denying food for a spiritual purpose—is perhaps one of the least practiced disciplines of all.

Fasting is a physical process that develops us spiritually. It's an act of physical denial that helps us gain so much more in our relationship with God and others.

In this week's video session, Kerry walks us through the purpose and power of fasting. Take a moment to read through the Scriptures on page 40 before watching "The Art of Restraint" (15:00). Then discuss the two questions designed as follow-up to the video on the Viewer Guide page.

SHOW VIDEO NOW.

VIEWER GUIDE

Included are two questions designed as follow-up to "The Art of Restraint." This time is set aside for discussion within the group about what they heard, how it affected them, and possible applications. These questions may be only a beginning. Feel free to begin the conversation by asking what thoughts, insights, or stories had the most impact on group members.

1. According to Kerry's message, what kind of hunger is stirred by fasting?

2. Kerry shares four benefits of fasting. Which resonates with you most? Circle it below. You'll have an opportunity to talk about why with other group members later in your group session.

   Fasting feeds my spirit.
   Fasting cleanses my body.
   Fasting reveals my sin.
   Fasting awakens my compassion.

BIBLICAL BACKGROUND

With music there is usually a story behind the song that helps listeners appreciate the heart and soul behind both the music and the lyrics. Scripture is no different. Below you'll find a brief story behind this week's Scripture intended to provide additional understanding and insight.

Throughout the history of Scripture, God has used the absence of something to help draw people closer to Himself. The Sabbath—the Jewish day of rest—is a denial of work. It is through refraining from work one day a week that we remember God is the King of the workplace and can provide for our needs.

With fasting, it is the denial of food. In both the Hebrew and Christian Scriptures the people of God use fasting for a variety of reasons, such as to show remorse or to call on God in a unique way to intercede on their behalf.

In Jesus' time fasting became a kind of "super discipline." It was something spiritual leaders used to publicly show how religious they were. As they fasted they would wail and not take care of themselves, becoming physically disheveled as a proof of piety. But Jesus called His followers to make fasting a private affair. The phrase "put oil on your head" was the ancient equivalent to hair spray or hair gel. In other words: take care of yourself. Act normal. Fasting is between you and God.

SCRIPTURE

[16] When you fast, do not look somber as the hypocrites do, for they disfigure their faces to show men they are fasting. I tell you the truth, they have received their reward in full. [17] But when you fast, put oil on your head and wash your face, [18] so that it will not be obvious to men that you are fasting, but only to your Father, who is unseen; and your Father, who sees what is done in secret, will reward you.
– Matthew 6:16-18

Then he said to them all: "If anyone would come after me, he must deny himself and take up his cross daily and follow me." – Luke 9:23

Jesus answered, "It is written: 'Man does not live on bread alone, but on every word that comes from the mouth of God.'" – Matthew 4:4

On that day they fasted and there they confessed, "We have sinned against the LORD." – 1 Samuel 7:6

SMALL-GROUP QUESTIONS

Over the next few pages you'll find discussion questions, material that may be used as additional discussion points, and a journal exercise for group members to complete away from the group.

"Fasting is a private discipline that brings a public reward."

1. Sometimes things are so meaningful that we need to share them. Other times they're meaningful *because* we don't share them. Why do you think this is the case?

2. Reread Matthew 6:16-18. Jesus is not saying that we've done wrong if people know we're fasting. It's all about our motive. Why do you think it is so important to guard our motives in fasting?

BACK DOOR BRAGGING

In the Emmy Award-Winning comedy *30 Rock*, Jenna is trying to help NBC page Kenneth get nominated to go to the Summer Olympics in Beijing, China:

> Kenneth: The personal essay is way harder than I thought, 'cause it's not in my nature to brag on myself.

> Jenna: Not even a back door brag?

> Kenneth: What's a back door brag?

> Jenna: Back door bragging is sneaking something wonderful about yourself in everyday conversation. Like when I tell people it's hard for me to watch *American Idol* 'cause I have perfect pitch. You try it.

> Kenneth: It's hard for me to watch *American Idol* because there's a water bug on my channel changer. (NBC, 2008)

Sometimes in our spiritual lives we are tempted to "back door brag." Yet when we do this, we rob ourselves of the value of doing something for its own sake rather than for the recognition of others.

3. Look back at question 2 on page 38. Out of the four benefits of fasting that Kerry mentions on the video, you circled the one that most resonates with you. What was your reason for choosing that particular benefit? Does it make you afraid of fasting? Excited about fasting? Confused about fasting? Explain.

"When it comes to fasting, my focus shouldn't be on the benefits of fasting; it should be on God."

4. It's possible to do the right thing for the wrong reasons. In your opinion, what are some wrong reasons to fast? What are some good reasons to fast?

5. What do you think might be the best ways to begin a fast? How about the best ways to end a fast?

**"Physical weakness shows a powerful spiritual truth:
you are weak but God is strong."**

6. How could fasting help you focus on the areas of life where you may think you're strong but you are actually weak?

7. How do you think a reminder of your weakness can help you in your relationship with God?

**"Desperate people are hungry people. ... When you hunger
for more of God you receive more of God."**

8. We often hear stories of people fasting in desperate situations—serious illness, dire financial circumstances, a desperate desire for children, and so on. Do you think this means that prayer is more powerful when we fast? Explain.

WISDOM FROM THE RECOVERY MOVEMENT

In 12-step programs they talk about the idea of hitting rock bottom. This is where a person has sunk so low in their lives that they have nowhere to go but up. Hitting rock bottom must happen in order for someone to begin genuinely pursuing the road to recovery. Rock bottom is a horrible place to be, but it is an important step toward health.

The key, they say, is raising your bottom. This is where we choose what our rock bottom is. It doesn't have to be divorce, joblessness, or finding ourselves in a gutter somewhere. It can be where we are right now in our lives. Raising the bottom means we're tired of finding the most tolerable form of misery and calling that happiness. When we fast, we're depending on God to help us raise our bottom. In the process we may be hungry for food, but we'll definitely be hungry for God.

9. You may or may not feel God calling you to fast right now. It will be different for everyone. But how might you use those emotions you experienced as a result of examining the benefits of fasting to be more sensitive to opportunities to fast in the future?

JOURNAL

What are some areas of your life where you would like to see your hunger for God increase—finances, relationships, job, church? Ask God to reveal others to you. Take some time to journal what you sense God is showing you.

YOU'RE UP

Fasting can be an incredible way to reinvigorate a stale faith. It's a strange paradox, but going without food can actually feed our souls and fill our spirits. Take the following thoughts with you throughout the next week:

- Fasting is meant to be a private act between us and God.

- Fasting helps us sense our spiritual hunger for God.

- Fasting can help cleanse our bodies.

- Fasting helps reveal to us our own sin.

- Fasting can help open us up to a deeper compassion for others.

During this next week, spend some time thinking and praying about how fasting might increase your awareness of your need for God. In the next session we will look at some pragmatic ways for you to begin fasting in your life. To prepare for the lesson, take a few minutes to read Judges 20:26-28; Ezra 8:21-23; Acts 13:3; and Matthew 5:6.

The Art of Emptying Yourself

Being hungry is a powerful experience: an ache in your stomach, the grumbling reminder of a need that's not being met. Knowing that food is only a few hours away can make it even worse. It's the same with thirst: the dry throat, your tongue sticking to the roof of your mouth. Nothing would be more satisfying than even just a drop of water.

When we go without, we become aware of our need. When we're aware of our need, it focuses us on what we truly care about. With fasting, we empty and open ourselves up to our longing for God and our desire for Him to move in our lives.

In this session we'll be talking about developing a plan for fasting and the options we have as we explore fasting as a tool for drawing closer to God.

WARM UP

When have you had to do without something you loved? Maybe it was food or water. Maybe the power went out, leaving you with no TV or air conditioning or heat. Maybe the battery died on your laptop or cell phone. Or maybe a friend moved away. What was that like?

What did you learn about yourself from that experience?

VIDEO SET UP

The information below sets up the video. It can be read aloud to the group, read by group members ahead of time, or group members can read the information silently while the facilitator sets up the video. Kerry ends this video session with a time of worship. Guide group members to participate as they feel most comfortable.

It's one thing to go without something because it's out of our control. It's something else entirely when we *intentionally* go without something for the sake of spiritual growth.

Many spiritual practices are daily affairs. Praying and spending time in the Word serve us best if we do them regularly. In fact, Scripture encourages us to "pray continually" (1 Thessalonians 5:17), to be constantly connected to God through conversation. If we tried the same thing with fasting, we wouldn't live very long. "Man does not live on bread alone" (Matthew 4:4), but bread eventually becomes necessary to sustain life. So when should we fast? How should we fast? For how long should we fast?

This week's video session walks us through a few different options as we explore fasting as a tool for drawing closer to God. Kerry lays out some biblical examples of fasting and the various goals fasting can have in our lives.

Take a moment to read through the Scriptures on page 54 before watching "The Art of Emptying Yourself" (12:13). Then discuss the two questions designed as follow-up to the video on the Viewer Guide page.

SHOW VIDEO NOW.

VIEWER GUIDE

Included are two questions designed as follow-up to "The Art of Emptying Yourself." This time is set aside for discussion within the group about what they heard, how it affected them, and possible applications. These questions may be only a beginning. Feel free to begin the conversation by asking what thoughts, insights, or stories had the most impact on group members.

1. Kerry shared some different ways to fast. What other ways of fasting are you aware of?

2. According to Kerry's message, when should we fast?

BIBLICAL BACKGROUND

With music there is usually a story behind the song that helps listeners appreciate the heart and soul behind both the music and the lyrics. Scripture is no different. Below you'll find a brief story behind this week's Scripture intended to provide additional understanding and insight.

The primary Scripture passages Kerry uses to highlight the different times we should fast represent three different times in Israel's history. Judges 20 highlights a conflict between the people of Israel and the people of Benjamin. Israel was losing a battle that God encouraged them to fight. On the first day they lost 22,000 men. The second day, 18,000. Before the third day the Israelites fasted and wept, seeking the counsel of God. God told them they would win, and on the third day they went into battle and did just that.

The second passage tells the account of Israel returning to their land after being held in captivity for generations by the Babylonians. Traveling was a dangerous affair and many of them were going to a place they had never been. But God gave them safe passage and protected them from enemies and bandits, allowing them to return home to begin building the kingdom of David anew.

In the third passage of Scripture, Saul and Barnabas had been chosen by God for a new task that would advance God's kingdom. The community of faith prayed and fasted for them, put their hands on them, and then sent them off on their mission.

Each passage is unique in the purpose and probably the kind of fast, yet each fast reveals the people of God humbly denying themselves as a way to connect with God and show their dependence on Him.

SCRIPTURE

---

²⁶ Then the Israelites ... went up to Bethel, and there they sat weeping before the LORD. They fasted that day until evening. ... ²⁸ The LORD responded, "Go, for tomorrow I will give them into your hands." – Judges 20:26,28

²¹ I proclaimed a fast, so that we might humble ourselves before our God and ask him for a safe journey for us and our children. ... ²³ So we fasted and petitioned our God about this, and he answered our prayer. – Ezra 8:21,23

After they had fasted and prayed, they placed their hands on them and sent them off. – Acts 13:3

Blessed are those who hunger and thirst for righteousness, for they will be filled. – Matthew 5:6

SMALL-GROUP QUESTIONS

Over the next few pages you'll find discussion questions, material that may be used as additional discussion points, and a journal exercise for group members to complete away from the group.

1. Matthew 5:6 speaks of "those who hunger and thirst." Someone who is really hungry and thirsty will devote all his or her energy to finding food and water. How does this compare to your hunger and thirst for God?

2. Do you see a difference between hunger and thirst? Explain.

FASTING IN THE BIBLE

The Bible provides us with multiple examples that all fasts are *not* created equal. Take a few minutes to check these examples out on your own.

1 night   Daniel 6:18

1 day   1 Samuel 7:6

3 days   Esther 4:16

7 days   1 Samuel 31:13

14 days   Acts 27:33-34

21 days   Daniel 10:3

40 days   Matthew 4:2

When should I fast? ... "When the odds are against me."

3. Has there ever been a time in your life when you felt like the odds were against you but God came through? What was that experience like?

4. What are some areas of your life where you feel like an Israelite, outnumbered and out of hope, getting beat by the tribe of Benjamin (Judges 20:26-28)?

When should I fast? ...
"When I need uncommon protection."

5. Who do you know who is in an especially vulnerable place right now? Take a moment to jot down some names.

6. What kind of protection could they use from God? What would it look like for you to fast about these things?

A PERSONAL BENT

I (Jason) am fortunate enough to have some very dear friends who are willing to fast and pray on my behalf. When I'm in the middle of a tough leadership decision, my friend Mark will fast for me. When I'm struggling in a particular relationship, Mark will cry out to God on my behalf—sometimes without telling me, other times over the phone.

Mark is one of those guys who knows that praying not only changes us but also has the power to change the future. I honestly don't know what I'd do without him. Mark inspires me to pray for myself and others. He's turned fasting and prayer into a form of serving others that I've personally seen bless him and those he serves.

When should I fast? …
"When I'm beginning a new endeavor."

7.   What new endeavors are you about to embark on in your life? Maybe you're coming into a new phase of life with regard to marriage or kids, or you're launching into a new career. Maybe it's a new service opportunity or a new church, or maybe the whole small group thing is new to you. What would it look like for you to fast about these things?

When should I fast? …
"When I need a major breakthrough."

8.   In his fourth point, Kerry uses the word "breakthrough" in reference to a time we should fast. How would you define that term for yourself? What would a major breakthrough look like in your life?

JOURNAL

This journaling opportunity is designed for group members to utilize at another time. They may choose to answer the question in the space provided or they may prefer to use the space and time to take a deep question or concern to God.

Whether or not you fast over the things the Lord has revealed to you this week, you can certainly pray for all these things in your life and the things that are in the lives of the others in your group. Take time to reflect on your list and to intentionally pray for everything that's weighing you down—whether it's feeling outnumbered, weak, vulnerable, beginning a new phase of life, or desperately needing a breakthrough.

YOU'RE UP

Consider fasting this week. Pray about it and use the tips below as your guide.

- Remember there are different types of fasts.

- Pick one of the things in your life that you feel you want to fast about, pick a type of fast, and then do it.

- Be ready for headaches and general grumpiness. But don't be afraid of it. Rather, lean into it as evidence of your dependence on God.

Next week we will begin talking about silence as a means of keeping our faith fresh and vibrant. To prepare for the lesson, read Isaiah 30:15; Lamentations 3:28; Psalms 46:10; 49:16-17; 62:1,5; and Ecclesiastes 5:7.

The Art of Margins

Silence is a powerful thing. It can be an intimate space between friends or an uncomfortable void between enemies. Silence exposes.

In the quiet moments our deepest fears, longings, and apathies rise to the surface. Our doubts, our lusts. Silence draws out our primal selves. Perhaps this is why we try so hard to avoid it with talking, music, television, Internet, texting, activity. Noise.

Yet no matter how loud our world gets, silence is waiting for us. To step into the deeper places of our souls. To listen to ourselves. To listen to God. To experience the calming of our inner storms.

In this week's session we'll look at how creating some margin in our lives for silence and solitude can help reduce stress and keep our faith fresh and vibrant.

WARM UP

Try not to spend too much time here, but let everyone answer the warm-up question. Getting group members involved early helps create the best small-group environment.

What are some things you typically do to fill silence?

VIDEO SET UP

The information below sets up the video. It can be read aloud to the group, read by group members ahead of time, or group members can read the information silently while the facilitator sets up the video. As you watch the video, encourage the group to follow Kerry's instruction to underline, circle, or interact with the key words in the passage.

We live in a world of constant noise. From the hum of the refrigerator to traffic. From the radio to television to people around us. And that's just audible noise. Noise can also be marketing and advertising, the silent fire hose of ideas that we are bombarded with at any given moment. Noise can even be the worry in our minds.

In our ears, before our eyes, in our heads. Noise is everywhere. It's almost impossible to have even a moment of complete silence. Yet Scripture names silence as one of the key spaces of spiritual development (Psalm 46:10; Matthew 11:15; Romans 10:17; James 1:19).

So how does silence help us grow spiritually? Why is it important? What does the Bible say about silence?

Take a moment to read through the Scriptures on page 68 before watching "The Art of Margins" (11:51). Then discuss the two questions designed as follow-up to the video on the Viewer Guide page.

SHOW VIDEO NOW.

VIEWER GUIDE

Included are two questions designed as follow-up to "The Art of Margins." This time is set aside for discussion within the group about what they heard, how it affected them, and possible applications. These questions may be only a beginning. Feel free to begin the conversation by asking what thoughts, insights, or stories had the most impact on group members.

1. According to Kerry, why is it so hard for us to stay silent?

2. What does silence say about our faith?

BIBLICAL BACKGROUND

With music there is usually a story behind the song that helps listeners appreciate the heart and soul behind both the music and the lyrics. Scripture is no different. Below you'll find a brief story behind this week's Scripture intended to provide additional understanding and insight.

All of the Scripture passages Kerry uses this week are poems of sorts. Isaiah's words were written in stanza form—some scholars even believe they were read to music. The Psalms, as mentioned before, were literally songs that would have been sung in the Jewish community in ancient times. Lamentations and Ecclesiastes are passionate prose—one of wailing and the other of intellectual struggle.

What's ironic is that all this music and poetry—all this noise—points to silence. Not all noise leads to more noise. Occasionally, if you listen to the noise, it will lead you to silence. Even in song the ancient Israelites celebrated the silence.

Silence, space, and rest all played crucial roles in Jewish spirituality, from observing the Sabbath to the practice of "sitting Shiva" (sitting in silence with those who are suffering). In these examples and more, God's ancient people knew that silence often spoke louder than words.

The same is true today.

SCRIPTURE

This is what the Sovereign LORD, the Holy One of Israel, says: "In repentance and rest is your salvation, in quietness and trust is your strength." – Isaiah 30:15

When life is heavy and hard to take, go off by yourself. Enter the silence. – Lamentations 3:28 (The Message)

Be still, and know that I am God; I will be exalted among the nations, I will be exalted in the earth. – Psalm 46:10

[1] For God alone my soul waits in silence; from him comes my salvation. ... [5] For God alone my soul waits in silence, for my hope is from him. – Psalm 62:1,5 (NRSV)

Many words are meaningless. Therefore stand in awe of God. – Ecclesiastes 5:7

[16] Do not be overawed when a man grows rich, when the splendor of his house increases; [17] for he will take nothing with him when he dies, his splendor will not descend with him. – Psalm 49:16-17

SMALL-GROUP QUESTIONS

Over the next few pages you'll find discussion questions, material that may be used as additional discussion points, and a journal exercise for group members to complete away from the group.

"The hardest thing to get Americans to do is nothing."
—Dallas Willard

1. Kerry mentions that noise can be damaging to our spiritual growth—he calls it "motion sickness of the soul." How might this be detrimental to our quality of life?

2. What happens to you internally when there's silence—in a conversation, late at night, early in the morning, and so on?

TECHNOLOGY AND CONTROL

All of us do little things to help us feel like we're in control. The most recent research on Twitter, Facebook, and e-mail is that the same chemical is released when we compulsively check those technologies as when a person takes illegal substances. [1] In short: the illusion of control can be incredibly addicting. Many people find themselves checking their e-mail dozens of times a day or checking their Twitter feed at any lull in the conversation or at any traffic light when driving through town. Scott Belsky, author of *Making Ideas Happen*, calls these twitches "insecurity work." [2] These insecure moments keep us from thinking deeply about anything. Like technological security blankets, we check e-mail and Facebook to somehow make us feel like we're in control. Yet often it accomplishes nothing other than adding to the noise of our lives.

"One of the reasons it's so hard for us to stay silent is because it makes us feel so helpless."

3. Often silence makes us feel weak and helpless, but Isaiah 30:15 says that strength can be found in the quiet. What are some things you try to control that are actually outside your control? How might silence help you deal more healthily with these things that are out of your control?

A PERSONAL BENT

I (Jason) used to reserve words like *awe* for experiences like the great Redwood trees or the Grand Canyon. I love how the grandeur of nature can make feeling small feel so good. Yet recently I've been finding silence and awe in more humble places. These days I've been going on short walks in my neighborhood. No phone. No iPod. Just me walking on the sidewalk, occasionally praying to God.

When I go on these walks, I notice the clouds. I notice the grass. I notice neighbors going about their business. It all happens without me and would continue to happen if I wasn't there. The grass would continue to grow. People would continue to love, live, and be late for soccer practice. It helps put my problems in perspective, and when I walk back into my house I involuntarily breathe a deep sigh of relief—like a weight has been lifted off my shoulders. I feel God saying, "I'm here." I feel wonder and gratitude for life. I think *awe* would be a very good word for that.

"Some of you have been really fighting [life] this week and it's time for you to stop and lay your head on your heavenly Father's chest and rest."

4. Sometimes it's easy to put our hope in ourselves—how hard we work, our own intelligence and capabilities. Reread Psalm 62:1,5. What do these verses say about hope?

5. What would be the benefit in your life of giving up the fight for control, putting less hope in yourself, and placing more hope in God?

"Silence recognizes the awe and wonder and mystery of God."

6. When was the last time you experienced awe? What was that like?

7. Ecclesiastes 5:7 contrasts "many words" with experiencing "awe." What do you think is the connection between silence and awe?

"When I'm speechless, God can speak to me."

8. What are some things that get in the way of us hearing God in our lives?

9. How might times of silence help us with that?

"Even if [I] don't hear Him say anything, ... I'm acknowledging that I'm not in control, but He is."

10. How can the simple act of being silent be a declaration in your heart that God is in control?

JOURNAL

This journaling opportunity is designed for group members to utilize at another time. They may choose to answer the question in the space provided or they may prefer to use the space and time to take a deep question or concern to God.

Take Kerry up on his challenge to spend 15 minutes a day in silence this week. As you do, use the space here to write down any worries, thoughts, feelings, or things to do that come to mind. Often writing these things down can help our minds focus more on God.

YOU'RE UP

As you pursue silence as a way to connect to God and revitalize your faith, keep the following in mind:

- Silence is one of the best ways to reduce stress.

- Don't get discouraged if practicing the discipline of silence is difficult for you at first.

- Silence is a great way to express our faith and trust in God.

- Listen for God, but don't be worried if He doesn't always speak on your timetable.

- Silence helps release us from our desire to control everything.

In the next session we will explore two more benefits of silence. To prepare for the lesson, take a few minutes to read James 1:19 and Proverbs 25:11.

1. Tommy Collison, "Why your internet addiction is simply biological," *SimplyZesty* [online] 25 Aug 2011, [cited 31 Aug 2011]. Available on the Internet: *www.simplyzesty.com.*
2. Scott Belsky, *Making Ideas Happen* (New York: Penguin Group, 2010), 104.

The Art of Silence

Silence can be the key to reducing our stress and is our individual declaration that God can be trusted. Silence can remind us of the very important reality that we're not in control. In this sense, silence can be liberating to us personally. Yet silence doesn't affect only us. Perhaps one of the greatest ways silence enhances our lives is in the area of relationships.

In this final session we'll talk about the role of silence in relationships. About how silence actually empowers communication and increases sensitivity.

WARM UP

Try not to spend too much time here, but let everyone answer the warm-up questions. Getting group members involved early helps create the best small-group environment.

One a scale of 1 to 10, how would you rate yourself as a listener?

I never stop talking. **1** ⋯⋯⋯⋯⋯⋯⋯⋯⋯⋯⋯⋯ **5** ⋯⋯⋯⋯⋯⋯⋯⋯ **10** I am the best listener on the planet.

What traits make you a great listener?

VIDEO SET UP

The information below sets up the video. It can be read aloud to the group, read by group members ahead of time, or group members can read the information silently while the facilitator sets up the video. As you watch the video, encourage the group to follow Kerry's instruction to underline, circle, or interact with the key words in the passage.

Have you ever been around people who simply don't listen? People who constantly interrupt or change the subject from what you are talking about? It's like they're just dying for you to stop speaking so they can share something about themselves or share an amazing, funny, or insightful thought that they have.

Have you ever *been* one of those people?

Most of us feel we're at least decent listeners. But the reality is that most of us are *not* decent listeners. Our own thoughts, opinions, and concerns can be the loudest noise in our lives. We need to learn how to create space for others in our world.

Silence plays a key role in creating this space. In being quiet we become more aware of each other. Sometimes we're silent so we can better listen to ourselves and to God. Other times we're silent so we can better listen to the needs of those around us.

In this week's video, Kerry walks us through the role of silence in relationships. Take a moment to read through the Scriptures on page 84 before watching "The Art of Silence" (12:51). Then discuss the two questions designed as follow-up to the video on the Viewer Guide page.

SHOW VIDEO NOW.

VIEWER GUIDE

Included are two questions designed as follow-up to "The Art of Silence." This time is set aside for discussion within the group about what they heard, how it affected them, and possible applications. These questions may be only a beginning. Feel free to begin the conversation by asking what thoughts, insights, or stories had the most impact on group members.

1. Who is the best listener in your life? Does he or she exhibit any of the traits Kerry mentioned in the video? Which ones?

2. Kerry shares that when we practice silence and solitude we are better able to move beyond our "I" problem so that we can focus on the needs of others. When we do this, what does Kerry say the Holy Spirit does for us?

BIBLICAL BACKGROUND

With music there is usually a story behind the song that helps listeners appreciate the heart and soul behind both the music and the lyrics. Scripture is no different. Below you'll find a brief story behind this week's Scripture intended to provide additional understanding and insight.

This week Kerry uses a passage from James's letter to followers of Jesus who were scattered throughout the Eastern world. The letter James wrote has become known as the "Proverbs of the New Testament." It's written in memorable and sometimes seemingly unrelated words of wisdom, primarily dealing in our relationships with others.

Kerry's other passage comes from the Old Testament Book of Proverbs—31 chapters of wisdom statements. Solomon wrote the majority of the verses but some were collected from various other cultures throughout the Middle East. In that sense, Proverbs represents the wisdom of God inherent in humanity, as Solomon was a student of wisdom, not merely a dispenser of it.

Both of these passages deal with our words (or lack thereof) and how they affect the people around us.

SCRIPTURE

My dear brothers, take note of this: Everyone should be quick to listen, slow to speak and slow to become angry.
– James 1:19

A word aptly spoken is like apples of gold in settings of silver. – Proverbs 25:11

SMALL-GROUP QUESTIONS

Over the next few pages you'll find discussion questions, material that may be used as additional discussion points, and a journal exercise for group members to complete away from the group.

"We get [James 1:19] turned around. We're quick to speak but slow to listen."

1. Why do you think it is so hard to listen sometimes?

2. Kerry says that many times "we hear but we don't really listen." How would you describe the difference between hearing and really listening?

IT'S ALL ABOUT ME

The word *narcissist* comes from the myth of Narcissus, a very handsome young man who was also very arrogant and rejected all those who loved him. His enemy (not coincidentally named Nemesis) took advantage of this and led Narcissus to a pool where he saw—and fell deeply in love with—his own reflection. As a result, Narcissus never left the reflecting waters and eventually died there.

When we focus only on ourselves, our selves begin to wither and die. It's when we can take care of ourselves and listen to and serve others that we begin to find the healthy kind of life and relationships that we long for.

3. Think about the people in your life. To whom do you listen best? With whom are you a more distracted listener? How do you think your listening habits affect your relationships with these people?

4. How might better listening change your relationships?

5. Read Proverbs 25:11 again. How would you describe a "word aptly spoken"?

6. How can silence help us learn which words are best suited and most responsive and which are not?

REEL TRUTH

Aaron Sorkin's *The Social Network* tells the story of Mark Zuckerberg and his quest to create Facebook. At the beginning of the film, Mark's girlfriend Erica breaks up with him. Mark goes home intoxicated and decides to blog about the break-up. He writes things he shouldn't have. Later his girlfriend says this to him:

> Erica: You called me a [witch] on the Internet, Mark.
>
> Mark: That's why I wanted to talk to you.
>
> Erica: On the *Internet*.
>
> Mark: That's why I came over.
>
> Erica: Comparing women to farm animals.
>
> Mark: I didn't end up doing that.
>
> Erica: It didn't stop you from writing it. As if every thought that tumbles through your head was so clever it would be a crime for it not to be shared. The Internet's not written in pencil, Mark, it's written in ink. (Columbia Pictures, 2010)

Even in verbal conversation, our words are written in "ink." No matter how badly we want to, we can never unsay something.

"The old proverb says, 'The man who opens his mouth shuts his eyes.' But when I get alone with God and I get silent before Him, He opens my eyes to see the needs of others."

7. Reread James 1:19. When was the last time you wish you had been "quick to listen" and "slow to speak"? Explain.

"Look beyond what's on the outside and see the hurt on the inside."

8. Take a few minutes and think about what's going on in the lives of the people around you—family, friends, coworkers. Kerry says, "One word spoken at the right time, in the right way, changes everything." How does it make you feel to know you might hold that "one word" that could make all in the difference for someone today?

9. How can you discover what that one word is and then use it to help meet a need this week?

JOURNAL

Sometimes we're hesitant to really listen to others or to be more aware of the needs of others because we're afraid. Maybe we're afraid we won't be equipped to help once we know their needs, afraid we will let someone down. Maybe we're afraid we don't really even know how to be silent and listen. Maybe we're afraid of not being in control. Or maybe in listening we're afraid of what we might discover about ourselves.

Spend some time this week writing about fears you feel regarding being a better listener and learning the art of focusing on others through silence. Ask God to show you what specific fears you need to work on to make you a better listener.

YOU'RE UP

Silence can be an incredible way to reinvigorate a stale faith and revitalize existing relationships. It can be the tool that God uses to liberate us from our narcissism and free us to serve Him and others. Take the following points as a challenge to consider this week:

- Silence empowers our communication with God and others.

- Silence helps us be quick to listen, slow to speak, and slow to become angry.

- Silence helps us use our words more aptly.

- Silence helps us become more aware of the needs of those around us.

- Silence can help free us from our narcissism.

Other titles in the Platform Series

Presence
by J.D. Greear
Discover whether you've been seeking God's presence or just His presents.

Have the Funeral
by James MacDonald
Take a closer look at the process of forgiveness, as well as the dangers of unforgiveness.

Life's Toughest Questions
by Erwin McManus
Does God care? Is there a hell? Explore these and other difficult issues in life.

Stand Against the Wind
by Erwin McManus
A study on character transformation. Become all God designed you to be.

The Controversial Jesus
by Erwin McManus
Re-introduce yourself to the Jesus who radically changed history and lives.

This collection of small group Bible studies features compelling video sermons from the platforms of some of today's most influential pastors. Visit us online to get more information and a free sample.

LifeWay | Small Group

More depth.
More meaning.
More life.

Ever feel like there's something in Bible study that others are getting but you're not? The more they carve and dig and analyze, the more lost you feel, the more distant and mysterious the big picture remains. But what if there were a way to put the pieces of Scripture together so that each slice seemed to be part of a single story? What if you could see the individual books and chapters united by common threads, held together by context and connections, an amazing meshing of God-inspired purpose extending far beyond time in both directions? You'd not only find the "more" in your Bible study, but more in your relationship with God, with each other, and with each day's experience of life. You'd enter the real adventure and find something about it that you never saw before. Something More.

Celebrate.

Learn.

Love.

Serve.

Building Biblical Community

Bill Donahue and Steve Gladen, with 50+ years and 30,000 groups in their experience, bring you the ideal resource for helping your church build community. Great with new or rebooting groups, or for staff or team retreats and community campaigns.

Easy-to-lead, it includes sound Bible teaching, group activities, core principles and practices, daily devotions, and leader tips that make your job more of a blessing than a burden.

Tired of trying to be a good Christian?

You give, you share your faith, you do all the things you're supposed to do as a disciple of Christ. But does it feel like something is still missing?

Find out what happens when you understand how to let the gospel work in your heart the way religion never has, or ever could. Through this eight-week study and the use of the "Gospel Prayer," you'll understand how to truly abide in Jesus. The natural results are passion, self-control, kindness, patience, and radical generosity. Your marriage can change. You can become more self-disciplined and less selfish. Not by concentrating on these things, but as a result of being captivated by the love of Christ.

GROUP DIRECTORY

NAME: _____

HOME PHONE: _____

MOBILE PHONE: _____

E-MAIL: _____

SOCIAL NETWORK (S): _____

NAME: _____

HOME PHONE: _____

MOBILE PHONE: _____

E-MAIL: _____

SOCIAL NETWORK (S): _____

NAME: _____

HOME PHONE: _____

MOBILE PHONE: _____

E-MAIL: _____

SOCIAL NETWORK (S): _____

NAME: _____

HOME PHONE: _____

MOBILE PHONE: _____

E-MAIL: _____

SOCIAL NETWORK (S): _____

NAME: _____

HOME PHONE: _____

MOBILE PHONE: _____

E-MAIL: _____

SOCIAL NETWORK (S): _____

NAME: _____

HOME PHONE: _____

MOBILE PHONE: _____

E-MAIL: _____

SOCIAL NETWORK (S): _____

NAME: _____

HOME PHONE: _____

MOBILE PHONE: _____

E-MAIL: _____

SOCIAL NETWORK (S): _____

NAME: _____

HOME PHONE: _____

MOBILE PHONE: _____

E-MAIL: _____

SOCIAL NETWORK (S): _____

NAME: _____

HOME PHONE: _____

MOBILE PHONE: _____

E-MAIL: _____

SOCIAL NETWORK (S): _____

NAME: _____

HOME PHONE: _____

MOBILE PHONE: _____

E-MAIL: _____

SOCIAL NETWORK (S): _____

NAME: _____

HOME PHONE: _____

MOBILE PHONE: _____

E-MAIL: _____

SOCIAL NETWORK (S): _____

NAME: _____

HOME PHONE: _____

MOBILE PHONE: _____

E-MAIL: _____

SOCIAL NETWORK (S): _____